Backyard Chickens for Beginners

ESSENTIAL STEP BY STEP GUIDE TO RAISING CHICKENS IN YOUR BACKYARD, CHOOSING A COOP, FEEDING AND CARE

JORDAN BRYCE

TABLE OF CONTENTS

INTRODUCTION   7

CHAPTER - 1
WHY RAISE CHICKENS   9

    BECOMING A 'CHICKEN PERSON'   11

    IMPORTANT NOTES ABOUT RAISING CHICKENS   13

CHAPTER - 2
HOW MUCH SPACE THE CHICKENS NEED
TO BE RAISED   15

CHAPTER - 3
CHOOSING A COOP   21

CHAPTER - 4
CHICKEN BREEDS AND HOW TO CHOOSE THE MOST
SUITABLE ONE   29

    COMMON BACKYARD BREEDS   30

    MORE CHALLENGING BREEDS FOR BACKYARD
    CHICKEN FARMING   33

    CONSIDERING OTHER CHICKEN BREEDS?   35

CHAPTER - 5
FEEDING THE CHICKENS   37

    ESSENTIALS FOR RAISING HEALTHY CHICKENS   37

    DIET   37

    HOW MUCH TO FEED   38

    WHAT TO FEED OR NOT FEED   39

CHAPTER - 6
TYPES OF ALIMENTATION   45

    TYPES OF FEED   46

THE NATURAL CHICKEN WATER — **48**

CHAPTER - 7
CARE AND CHICKEN MAINTENANCE — **53**

CHAPTER - 8
DISEASES — **57**

BUMBLEFOOT — 57

VENT PROLAPSE — 57

EGG YOLK PERITONITIS — 58

EGG BOUND — 59

MAREK'S DISEASE — 59

FROSTBITE — 60

CHAPTER - 9
BEHAVIOR AND CHICKEN PSYCHOLOGY — **61**

PECKING ORDER — 61

CHICKEN CALLS — 63

BABY TALK — 64

MAMA CALLS — 64

ANGRY BIRDS — 64

CHICKCHAT — 65

SOUND THE ALARM! — 65

ROOSTER DYNAMICS — 66

BAD BEHAVIOR: EGG EATING — 67

CHAPTER - 10
    EGGS   **69**

    WHEN DO HENS START LAYING EGGS?   69

    EGG COLLECTION   70

    CLEANING EGGS   70

    PROBLEMS WITH EGGS   71

    EGG BINDING   72

    HOW AGE EFFECTS LAYING   72

CHAPTER - 11
    CHICKEN LAWS   **75**

    WHAT TO EXPECT   76

    CHANGING LAWS   77

CHAPTER - 12
    TIPS FOR RAISING CHICKENS   **79**

    TOP FIVE THINGS YOU NEED TO BE AWARE OF WHEN RAISING CHICKENS   80

    RAISE CHICKEN LIKE AN EXPERT!   83

CONCLUSIONS   **85**

Introduction

Doing anything for the first time can present itself as a daunting task, but the good thing about raising backyard chickens is you don't have to do everything all at once. Everything you do will come in certain preordained steps, typically you have to have one stage of the process done before you advance on to the next. Allow me to lay out all of them for you right now. Because you don't have to be a chicken, you just need a few tips to get you started!

Handling Potential Permits and Fees

Depending on where you live you may have to pay a fee in order to get your permit to raise chickens. In some locales, the permit fee is as little as five dollars. If you have the bare minimum of pocket change, in most places you can get yourself an official permit to raise chickens. Along with this permit often comes a signed agreement to allow your property to be subjected to annual inspections.

This is not a big deal; it usually simply entails one local animal control officer swinging by the premise to take a look at your chicken coop. After a few minutes of a cursory inspection, the officer will give you the all clear and be on his way. The sooner you understand how to handle potential permits and fees; the sooner you can get started on raising your chickens.

Know How Many Chickens You Can Legally Have

Urban areas mostly require backyard chicken farmers to have no more than 3 or 4 chickens. But if you live in an agricultural area, you will be allowed to have twice that many. Once you know how many chickens you can have, you can start preparing your coop accordingly. You won't know how big to build it after all, until you know just how many chickens will be inside the coop to begin with. Check with your city board or council to find out just how many chickens you can legally have.

Be Aware of Distance Regulations

Distance relations can be a bit of a nuisance at times, but these are laws that were created with the welfare of your chickens—as well as your most immediate neighbors—welfare in mind.

Some towns, however, do not have the clearest of restrictions in place, so you really have to check with the local powers that be to figure out how far away you need to keep your chickens. The local administrators can pull up official ordinance that state exactly how far away your chicken coop needs to be from neighboring property lines and local businesses. You may find that your area does not have any such restrictions at all, but you have to ask first.

Figure Out Zoning Rules

Before you get your chickens, you should educate yourself on the zoning rules of your community. If your property is zoned to be an "agricultural" region, you shouldn't have any trouble having chickens at all. But for those who are zoned as "residential, business, or urban" you will have to consider the applicable zoning rules that apply. The sooner you do so, the sooner you can get that chicken coop up and running.

Chapter - 1
WHY RAISE CHICKENS

Believe it or not, there are other reasons why you should think about raising chickens for eggs—right in your own backyard. Of course, the best reason is the eggs.

Flavorful and fortified eggs

People who raise chickens for eggs say fresh eggs are incomparable to the eggs you find in a supermarket. They're much more flavorful, fresh and have a better taste than the eggs you're used to eating. You can even see the difference in the yolk—fresh eggs have yolks that are a healthier looking orange than the pale yellow seen in store-bought eggs.

For health reasons, fresh eggs are better, too. Organically cultivated eggs are said to have higher amounts of omega-3 fatty acids and vitamin E, while having much lower levels of cholesterol than store-bought eggs.

Chickens are personable pets

Besides the eggs, the chickens themselves make great pets. Chickens are actually pretty personable. Like many animals, they have their own personalities—and, they'll make sure you know it, too! Given the types of chicken breeds out there (we'll go into more detail about that, too), you'll also be exposed to the beauty of having a flock of chickens at your home. In other words, they make great pets!

Chickens afford 'parents' sustainability

Another interesting thing about having chickens in your backyard is the sustainability. Having egg-laying hens affords you some sustainability, since you don't have to rely on heading to the supermarket to get eggs. You also don't have to worry about getting store-bought compost for your garden, since your chickens will produce waste that's easily convertible into compost, essentially fortifying your yard with all-natural compost.

They help produce rich compost and keep the yard tidy

So, how good is all-natural compost? Compost helps reduce your ecological footprint, introducing a pile of compost to your yard that's nitrogen-rich and, frankly, so rich that it helps enrich and 'feed' your yard. Chicken manure is an excellent resource for building a nutrient-rich compost pile. Eggshells, too, also work incredibly well in a compost pile, adding in essential nutrients from the shells that eventually transfer into the soil itself.

Chickens even help keep your grass from getting unruly. They like nibbling and eating grass, among other foods—such as garden pests! Yes, they even eat bugs that might harm your garden, such as beetles, grubs and earwigs. Some breeds even consume small mammals like moles! Tenured chicken breeders have also suggested feeding chickens some of your leftover food, especially the foods they can safely eat. So, don't feel guilty about feeding them 'from your plate!'

They're a joy to raise

Of course, the most important part is keeping your chickens running around freely. And, when you keep them in their large chicken run, they'll have enough space to, well, do as they please. Chickens are said to love ranging freely around a yard, so if you want to keep them happy (and yourself happy), make sure they have the space to feel free.

Believe it or not, chickens are pretty low maintenance, too. They don't need that much walking, grooming or feeding. Of course, you'll have to make sure their feeders and water container are full throughout the week. You'll also have to make sure their bedding is clean and tidy and gather eggs when needed. But chickens are ultimately self-sustaining birds—as long as you let them take care of themselves, you'll only have to look after their health.

All of the aforementioned reasons are pretty good reasons why you should think about raising backyard chickens. Though, we're wondering something about you, this time. Are you a chicken person?

Becoming A 'Chicken Person'

There are dog people. Cat people. Even reptile people and fish people. But, are you a chicken person? That is, a person that adores chickens (and possibly other birds) to the point of raising them right at home.

It might sound a little ridiculous, but you really have to adore chickens to raise them. Or, any pet, really. Though, with the work that it takes to raise chickens in a backyard, you have to love them to handle the management aspect of the process.

Chickens are pretty uncommon as pets. They're even more uncommon as a resource of food (eggs) right at home. As an uncommon pet, they're not exactly the hardest pets to raise.

Think about it:

If you love chickens, you'll want to raise them. Raising chickens isn't, as they say, for the faint of heart. There's a lot of management that goes into running a chicken coop in your backyard, including work that needs to be done throughout the week.

If you don't like chickens, you're definitely not going to want to handle that part of the process. As with any pet, don't take care of them if you can't care for them. The care you put into taking care of your chickens will reflect on them and may even affect their health in the long run. You don't want that.

Of course, raising any pet takes time. With chickens, you'll have to devote a significant portion of your time ensuring they're okay. Cleaning their coops and removing eggs each day. Shoveling chicken manure into the compost pile and putting other waste (like eggshells) into the pile, too.

Most of these tasks can be done within minutes, usually at least 10 to 20 minutes of your day, and it all adds up. Most chicken caretakers spend up to an hour or so per month managing their chickens. Some spend more time, only because they truly adore their chickens. If you can't manage to have enough time to care for them, you might not be able to raise chickens in your backyard.

That brings up another point. Your backyard. If you don't have a large enough backyard, you probably won't be able to house your chickens. Although we've mentioned this before, it's pretty important to know.

Chickens actually don't need that much space. But, when you consider how active chickens are, they need all the space they can get. Chickens are foragers by nature and enjoy wandering about the expanse of your yard, doing the things they like to do—foraging, eating and just mingling about. They also like picking and scratching at the ground, which has the beneficial effect of aerating soil in your yard.

A tight yard might be too small for housing several chickens. In fact, chickens are known to make a small yard into a 'dust bowl,' or turning it into a rather shabby looking place. If you have a larger yard, their 'work' can turn it into a healthier looking yard. They preen and eat grasses and weeds, yard pests and scratch the soil—all of that activity can benefit your yard if you provide them enough space.

Important Notes About Raising Chickens

We've provided some pretty good reasons to raise chickens, though there's a bit of a catch. You can't raise chickens in your backyard without knowing the legalities of it all.

Some towns and cities don't allow residents to raise chickens in their backyard. If they do, you may need to check the health board and zoning board regulations in your city to learn more about keeping uncommon animals like chickens as pets.

If your town or city does allow 'residential chickens,' note that you may need to check local waste disposal regulations before getting them. Other matters like property lines, coop-related regulations, local noise regulations and other local laws are important to research long before getting your chickens.

Speaking of noise regulations, you might have neighbors if you live in a residential neighborhood. Most people do. So, you'll have to keep your neighbors in mind if you plan to keep chickens in your home. The noise, the smell and even the possibility of some of your chickens wandering too far from home are things you should keep in mind.

If you do have friendly neighbors, it doesn't hurt to talk to them about your intentions for raising chickens in the neighborhood. Some people even end up being the local 'egg seller,' thanks to their neighbor's acceptance of their chickens!

Remember that there's nothing 'free' about raising chickens, either. Both time and money are required to successfully raise chickens in your backyard. Of course, that means there are no shortcuts, either. As long as you keep that in mind, you'll be pretty successful at raising your own chickens.

Chapter - 2
HOW MUCH SPACE THE CHICKENS NEED TO BE RAISED

The term "chicken coop" has different meanings to different people. In this booklet, the "coop" is the structure where chickens go to spend the night. In addition to this coop, they will have some kind of outdoor run area, whether this is free range or enclosed. Some people mix these two areas together and call them both a "coop". To keep things clear, I will refer to the inside area as the "coop" and the outside area as the "run".

Happy chickens lay lots of eggs, so it is in your basic self-interest to keep them happy. Happy chickens need a minimum of four (4) square feet of coop space per bird, plus a run area of at least ten (10) square feet per bird. I base these numbers on the recommendations of Gail Damerow in Storey's Guide to Raising Chickens.

If there is no outside run area, then chickens need ten (10) square feet of coop space per bird. I will ignore this last suggestion, because you should not be keeping chickens if you cannot provide them with some outside space to move around in (whether this space is free range or in an enclosed pen). So, let's look at the first number: four (4) square feet of coop space per bird.

If your chickens are outside most of the time, basically using the coop just for sleeping and laying eggs, then four (4) square feet per bird is adequate. If chickens are kept in the coop for long periods when they cannot go outside, especially if you are trying to overwinter them inside, then they need extra coop space. The proper coop size also depends on the size of the chickens you are keeping. Bantams are much smaller than standard birds, so you can fit more of them in any given coop.

Even for standard birds, there is a big difference between an eight-pound Orpington and a five-pound Ameracauna hen. For medium-sized breeds like Ameracauna, I would feel more comfortable using the minimum size, while a flock of larger birds like Orpys could get pretty crowded with only four (4) square feet per bird. Tight conditions make for more fighting and risk of disease, so give them plenty of space.

Let's apply the four (4) square foot recommendation in the small backyard setting. Two hens would need a coop of at least eight (8) square feet, say two feet by four feet (2' x 4'). Three hens would need twelve (12) square feet, which might be a three by four-foot (3' x 4') coop. Four hens would need sixteen (16) square feet, which could be accomplished with either a four by four (4' x 4') square coop or a more rectangular three and a half by five (3.5' x 5'). This should not seem like a lot of space, since it is only a few inches larger than a standard-sized bathtub.

But the outdoor run area will take up the most space. The run area should provide at least ten (10) square feet of space for each chicken. Again, this is a minimum, which I would increase by a few feet if the feeder and waterer take up part of the space. So, let's crack the numbers again to see how this looks for a city dweller with a small backyard. Two hens would need a run space of at least twenty (20) square feet, perhaps three and a half feet by six feet (3.5' x 6'). Three hens would need thirty (30) square feet, either in a block of around five by six feet (5' x 6') or a strip such as three by ten feet (3' x 10').

Four hens would need forty (40) square feet, which you could create with a five by eight-foot (5' x 8') block or a four by ten foot (4' x 10') plot.

Do not ignore side yards as possible run areas. At my daughter's former school, which has two hens we donated, they keep the chickens in a coop attached to a long, narrow fenced strip next to the building. This pen, which the children can walk inside to play with the chickens and harvest eggs, is only about three feet wide, but at least 20 feet long. It could have been used as a long flower bed at one time.

At only three feet wide, I may never have seriously considered this for a chicken area, but it provides these two hens with plenty of run space. There are some shelves and an old rabbit hutch on one end, which were turned into an open-sided coop. The coop is covered from the rain and the climate is quite mild, so the chickens do not complain that it is only enclosed on only three sides. Their wild ancestors slept in trees, not small houses.

The run space does not need to be square or rectangular, though that is usually the easiest way to go. In the run area, make sure to have some perches they can roost on during the day; I use one-inch thick dowels or garden stakes, placed 2-3 feet off the ground. The main concern with the run is to keep it covered with plenty of mulch or bedding. Chicken manure makes the soil toxic very quickly, but this can be balanced (and odors nearly eliminated) with the addition of some carbon-rich mulch/bedding.

A thick layer of straw, leaves, shredded paper, or sawdust as bedding will help the chicken manure decompose naturally and create a balanced compost. Keep at least a few inches of this mulch on the ground at all times and change it every couple of months. Old chicken bedding with manure can go right into a compost bin or tumbler, where it will decompose and make a rich addition to your garden soil the next year.

My chickens have a fully enclosed run which is a little larger than this minimum size. I built this enclosure with a frame of 1 ½ x 1 ½ inch wooden stakes, covered with half inch wire mesh that is secured by large staples. Part of the run is shaded by the coop, which sits on top of it, providing some protection from the elements on hot or rainy days. Even the bottom of the run is lined with poultry wire, though the soil and mulch on top of it are deep enough that the chickens never scratch down to the wire.

The coop is open to the run, so that the chickens can use it every day. If I am away from home, this is where they spend the day. I do not need to close anything up at night because the coop and run are sealed. Predators and pests (such as raccoons and rats) cannot get in.

When I am home, there is a gate I can open to give them more outdoor space. Attached to the gate is an extended run area behind my raised vegetable beds and under some fruit trees. It is lined with temporary plastic fences to keep the chickens out of my vegetable garden, and since I do not consider these fences very strong, I only let the chickens out into this area when I am home (which may only be an hour or two in the morning or evening).

These fences, in turn, are attached to a third run area, which is made from a couple of temporary dog fences. I move this around, sometimes letting them into part of the yard to eat weeds and bugs, and other times directing them onto one of my raised beds, which they can scratch in for a few months at a time. They aerate and fertilize the soil, which I often cover with compost or mulch that they dig in for me. Here is a picture of them doing their thing in part of a raised bed, which has a movable, temporary fence protecting the vegetables and blueberries.

The chickens love to take dust baths in this deep soil also, which is an important part of their hygiene and pest protection. A month or two after letting them into the bed, they will have it thoroughly transformed (though I cannot plant in the soil until their manure breaks down a bit, say 6-12 months, since the ammonia needs to convert to plant-usable nitrogen). After a hawk dropped in one day and tried to attack a full-sized hen, I covered the extended run with plastic bird netting. Putting this on only took a few minutes because it does not need to be secured too well; the mere sight of it seems to keep chickens in and hawks out.

Chapter - 3
CHOOSING A COOP

At initially, it appears to make great sense that purchasing chickens that have actually currently laid eggs for a year would be an exceptional concept. However, there are too numerous unfavorable problems for considering this to be a perfect choice. These chickens can cost more and have a number of other drawbacks. Purchasing second-year chickens suggest you will not get the greatest quality or optimum production from your chickens.

Beginning with day-old chicks will need you to get a brooder that will keep them warm and comfy for their very first numerous weeks till they are big enough to live out-of-doors in a portable chicken tractor or hen home. This indicates you will be needed to get a brooder, triggering your expenses to climb up. Plus, it indicates you will require to supply unique care and attention to your brand-new chicks if you desire them to endure to maturity.

You can develop a little flock of laying hens either by hatching eggs on your own or purchasing living chickens. If you are a novice at yard chicken raising, you will most likely desire to get living hens as a replacement for hatching eggs.

Yard chicken raising can be easy, satisfying, and lucrative. The very first thing you ought to do is to purchase or develop your own chicken arks, likewise, called chicken tractors, or hen homes. After you have your portable chicken ark or hen home and the extra fundamental products, you can continue to purchase your flock.

For the yard chicken raising novice, there are three methods to select from if you are going, beginning with live hens. Second, you have the choice to obtain begun pullets that are simply under five months old. And 3rd, you can get chickens that have actually currently laid eggs one season and are all set to begin their 2nd term of laying.

Plus, you will not have the supplemental expense of a chicken brooder and will not require to invest as much time caring for the pullets due to the fact that they will be put straight into your chicken tractor or hen home. Getting began pullets is the most convenient way for the yard chicken raising novice to get begun in their brand-new pastime.

A yard chicken cage is not just a structure were your chickens will live in; it likewise secures them from relentless animals and from the weather condition. Yes, you can purchase a yard chicken cage; however, the expense will skyrocket high.

1. Get a strategy. First of all, it is important that you have prepared for your yard chicken cage. A couple of years ago, it would be tough to discover such strategies; however, thanks to the web, you can get them at the convenience of your own house.

If you are a knowledgeable carpenter or an overall newbie, the yard chicken cage strategies must fit everyone's' requirements. Chicken home strategies are a vital tool; without them, it would generally cost you a lot of time and a lot of aggravation.

2. Material On the strategy or on the guideline, it ought to be no issue for you to discover what products you require to utilize for your yard hen home. More than likely, you will require some kind of wood, chicken wire, insulation, doors, and windows.

3. Size Then, it is necessary to understand how huge your yard chicken home require to be. Chickens require a 4 square feet area. If you just have a little lawn, you can make it 2 feet, however, do not go lower then that. Otherwise, they do not have sufficient space to set to produce eggs or to sleep excellent.

Contrary to common belief, you do not need to be a farmer and even own a cattle ranch to delight in the advantages of raising chickens. Chickens do not need a great deal of area to live conveniently and can adjust to and grow in practically any environment as long as they have a correct house. This enables typical individuals, like you and me, to develop portable chicken cages and raise a flock of chickens in their own yard.

Raising backyard chickens is not just a fulfilling experience. However, it can likewise conserve you cash! You will get to delight in the advantages of fresh, natural eggs on an everyday basis, which can be taken in plain or utilized in any of your routine cooking. Raising chickens is a sensible and budget-friendly alternative for anybody with a little backyard, thanks to the fantastic idea of portable chicken cages.

Portable chicken cages are a terrific alternative for house owners without a great deal of land since:

They are affordable.

They are durable, keeping chickens safe from extreme components and outdoors predators.

They are small in size and do not use up much space.

They are light-weight and can be transferred to a fresh spot of lawn every day.

They are simple to construct, even for beginners!

Building a Backyard Chicken Coop on a Budget

I have actually been examining many of the items for many years and have actually discovered that not all strategies are of equivalent worth or equivalent interest to everybody. Some strategies are constructed for the specialist carpenter, while others do not use sufficient details for the newbie. I am a real follower of acquiring an excellent set of strategies, if you can discover a terrific set of complementary strategies by all imply, proceed and attempt it. However, from my experience, it is not readily available to the typical individual. Unless you understand somebody that has actually experienced developing a yard chicken cage, you will ultimately discover yourself scratching your head, questioning what failed.

Everybody is attempting to exact the same cash and time, and I will be the very first to state that these are my two most significant issues when beginning a brand-new task. Money and time are something you can never ever have enough of, which each and everybody among us is defending more of. I'm here to assist you in choosing what the finest set of chicken cage structure strategies is for somebody with time and cash issues

Is the typical individual mindful of the city regulations concerning constructing a yard chicken cage? Do you recognize there are various designs of cages, such as portable ones and fixed ones?

The typical individual most likely recognizes things like area, food, and routine cleansing are the essential things to stress about. Does the typical individual understand how much area, how much food, and what kind of food and how to construct a cage for the simplest upkeep and clean up? Most likely not.

Developing a cage is not a challenging job however there are numerous aspects that enter into constructing one that requires to be taken into factor to consider, and if you have not skilled raising chickens previously, you might not even understand what need to be an issue up until it's too late, which obviously suggests more work and more cash in the long run.

A great set of strategies will review all of the fundamental issues concerning these concerns and use you much, a lot more in return. For a little charge, your future issues will be gotten rid of, making your brand-new task an enjoyable and interesting experience for the entire household, rather of ending up being a continuous job of life and find out experiences.

How to Build A Chicken Coop For Beginners

When constructing a chicken cage is the area, one thing to bear in mind. The more additional area the birds have, the much better. Chickens with extra area carry out much better than those kept in little cages.

In truth, it ought to essentially have two doors, one for people and another little door for chickens. If your cage is high enough off the ground, you might require building a ramp from the chicken door to the flooring.

Considering keeping some chickens in your yard? Well, then you are going to require a chicken cage. Here's a brief guide on how to construct a chicken cage for beginners.

To get the hens utilized to nesting in packages, put them on the flooring for the 1st two weeks then move them up seventeen to nineteen inches.

The last thing your cage is going to desire is a door.

To make them lay their eggs in the nests, make sure the nests remain in a dark location far from the primary activity of the cage. The essential element here is to ensure you have adequate space for all of your chickens as the chickens on the bottom end of the chain of command will get pressed away if there's not adequate area.

A guideline of thumb is to provide 2 to 3 square feet of space per chicken. Make sure the cage is effectively aerated. This is needed to keep the chickens from overheating in the summer season and freezing in the winter.

In the winter season, you can stack hay bales around the north wall of the cage. Predators might dig and attempt under the cage to get in. Ensure there's enough area for all the chickens on the roost.

These pointers need to assist you quickly construct a budget-friendly and appealing chicken cage that is simple to preserve and healthy for chickens to lay eggs regularly.

You might be on a tight budget plan, believing that the strategies are a location where you might make some cost savings. Let me impart some more clearness into it.

Many people do not recognize the following:

1. That expert chicken cage structure strategies consider the well-being of your chickens through the addition of primary elements, which are accountable for the security of your chickens in addition to their durability, wellness, and health. Chickens sweat, so the cage style supplies arrangements for ventilation in order to manage temperature level inside the cage to finest fit your chickens;

2. Through being attempted and checked many times, expert cage structure strategies are created in a manner that streamlines the whole cage structure procedure, minimizing tension levels and conserving you cash;

If it is simply you, constructing the cage for the very first time, there are thousand and one legitimate factors to select a great set of expertly developed chicken cage strategies. The run and the cage are your chicken's sanctuary, and they are your chicken's house. Professionals think that the chicken cage alone accounts for as much as 3/4 of your chicken's health and wellness.

Well developed chicken home a joint with the chicken run comes with arrangements for lighting, ventilation, and insulation in addition to setting down bars, dust baths, and nesting boxes. In the exact same breath, all of this ends up being simple with a great set of structure strategies as expertly developed chicken cage strategies offer arrangements for these primary requirements.

Here is an example of somebody who believed he would conserve cash by not utilizing the strategies when developing his very first ever chicken home: a customer of mine lost all their chickens to a skunk since his chicken home was not effectively protected, making it possible for the skunk to get access one night and eliminate all of his chickens.

Choosing on the number of chickens and the cage size is a crucial preliminary action. There is a choice that optimizes the usage of small yard areas by constructing the cage and the run in a method that locations sleeping location on the upper level whilst the chicken run is positioned on the premises below.

Chapter - 4
CHICKEN BREEDS AND HOW TO CHOOSE THE MOST SUITABLE ONE

Many chicken breeds are strikingly beautiful. However, if you rely on beauty alone as you choose birds for your flock, it can quickly lead to problems. Each breed has its own unique characteristics. Factors like how large the birds are and their activity level play a major role in how much space they need.

Housing too many chickens in a small area can cause a high level of ammonia that is unhealthy and unsanitary—for you and your birds. Additionally, the male-to-female ratio should be considered as you think about size. Below, we'll discuss some of the more common birds for backyards. Then we'll discuss a few of the rarer options, should you decide you want to collect chickens.

Something to remember is that there is no one-size-fits-all description for these birds. All descriptions are generalized, and each chicken will vary depending on its environment and upbringing. You should expect your chickens to have a unique personality that goes along with their breed description, though some birds have personalities far from what you are expecting from their descriptions.

Common Backyard Breeds

When you are beginning as a chicken farmer, it can be helpful to start with one of these more common backyard breeds. Most of these have been selected for their even temperament. They are easier to take care of than some other chicken breeds for this reason and you are less likely to have fighting among your birds.

Ameracauna Chickens

True Ameracauna chicks are known for their ability to lay blue eggs. However, they are a rare breed native to South America. In North America, the birds referred to as Ameracauna chickens or "Easter Eggers" are descendants of hens from Chile. They migrated to America in the 1970s.

The Ameracauna variety is a good choice for egg laying. They have exuberant personalities and lay pretty eggs in various shades of green, blue, and cream.

Leghorn Chickens

If you have a large flock, Leghorn chickens may not be a good choice. They are a good starter bird, but they startle easily and generally do not have calm personalities. People that do choose these chickens often choose them for their egg-laying, as they lay around 280 white eggs each year. Leghorn chickens are ideal for warmer climates.

Orpington Chickens

Buffs are the most common Orpington variety of chickens. They are usually gentle-natured birds with big, fluffy features. Orpington chickens serve two purposes. Even though they were originally bred for meat, they tolerate cold climates well and lay eggs through the winter, making them a great dual-purpose bird.

Families with young children may also appreciate these gentle birds as pets. They tolerate handling well and allow themselves to be picked up. As they are more docile birds, they are easier targets for predators. You will generally want to keep these birds in a fenced-in area to keep them safe.

Star Chickens

This variety is not formally recognized as a breed, but they are a common hybrid chicken. Varieties include the RedStar and BlackStar chickens. One major benefit of this bird is the distinct difference in the coloring between male and female chicks, which is good if you are trying to keep the number of roosters on your farm balanced to the number of females.

The calm personality of Star chickens makes them a good choice for new bird farmers. They are also productive, laying about 260 brown eggs annually.

Sussex Chickens

Sussex chickens are another popular choice for families. They have curious and friendly personalities that make them very pet-like. The Sussex chicken is an English breed and was once the most common for meat across Britain. They have brown plumes with white specks. This unique pattern is pretty to look at, but it also serves as camouflage in the wild.

New Hampshire Red Chickens

New Hampshire Reds are more commonly chosen for meat than egg purposes, but they also make a good dual-purpose bird. Their early maturity means you can choose birds to use as meat more frequently.

These are descendants of Rhode Island Red chickens. They have a wide range of personalities, with some being more aggressive and being focused on the pecking order and others being more relaxed. They are a good choice for someone who is frequently keeping a watchful eye on their chickens. Otherwise, you may want a more docile breed.

Brahma Chickens

Brahma chickens are popular for their calm nature. Those these birds are quite large; they are also quite docile. They are a good choice among chicken farmers in the north, as the hardiness and large size of these chickens makes them a good choice in damp or cold climates. Part of this is due to their feathered feet, which keep them warm.

Brahma birds were originally developed for meat production, as they only lay an average of 150 brown eggs each year. However, their personality makes them an excellent choice as a pet.

Jersey Giant Chickens

As the name suggests, these chickens are quite large. These are dual-purpose birds, laying around 260 brown eggs each year. Their giant size comes along with a calm, tame personality that makes them perfect as a beginner chicken. Jersey Giant chickens are the biggest bird of the pure breeds and they come in white, black, and blue varieties.

Wyandotte Chickens

Also known as American Sebright chickens, these pretty birds are known for laying large quantities of eggs while remaining good meat birds. Wyandotte chickens lay brown eggs and thrive in a wide range of weather conditions. They also have docile personalities and striking coats. The most common birds of this variety have silver-laced feathers.

Plymouth Rock Chickens

This attractive breed's most common variety is the Barred Rock chicken, which has black and white stripes. These birds are native to Massachusetts and are another dual-purpose bird. Their wide range of purposes, attractiveness, and gentle personality once made the Plymouth Rock chicken the most common breed across America. Other varieties include White Buff, Partridge, Columbian, Black,

Blue, Penciled, and Silver.

The Plymouth Rock bird is friendly and can do well when confined, however, they will be happier with a chance to roam freely. You'll have to be careful about overheating in warm climates.

Australorp Chickens

This dual-purpose chicken can lay up to 250 brown eggs for the year. Native to Australia, these chickens come in varieties of white, black, and blue. They have friendly personalities and are docile birds. Another benefit is their ability to forage, which allows them to hunt for treats and insects on the ground around their coop.

More Challenging Breeds for Backyard Chicken Farming

The breeds suggested above generally have calm dispositions. These chickens are a little harder to care for. Something to remember is that not all more active chicken breeds are trouble. In fact, you may find you love the personalities of your more active birds. Additionally, by spending more time with your chickens when they are young, you can help them develop a calmer temperament.

Rhode Island Red Chickens

The Rhode Island Red chicken is known for producing a high quantity of eggs, though they have been common on poultry farms too. They are active birds that will require a lot of space and a higher female-to-male ratio.

Some chicken farmers appreciate the Rhode Island Red chickens' docile personality, especially if they have been close with the chick when they were young. However, others bully amongst themselves or bully other breeds. Their bullying habits can be too much for a novice chicken farmer.

Polish Chickens

Polish chickens are often targeted by other breeds because of their feathered crest. Additionally, the feathers on their crest may grow so long that they cannot see clearly through their feathers. You'll need to keep a close eye on Polish chickens and regularly trim their crest feathers, otherwise, they'll likely be bullied by more dominant birds.

Silkies

Silkies have soft, delicate feathers that make for an adorable bird. Many people consider them the teddy bear of the chicken world. Even though it can be tempting to add these cute chicks to your collection, they are often pushed around and picked on by other breeds. Silkies are very submissive and require a breeder that can keep a close eye on them, especially on larger chicken farms or farms where you have a lot of breeds.

Japanese Bantams

The Japanese Bantam chicken has a calm nature and is easy to tame. However, they are not good breeders as about 25% develop a gene that stops them from hatching. These are good brooders and are liked for their long, luxurious coat of feathers.

Cochin Chickens

Cochins are poor flyers, so they are a good choice if you have a shorter fence. They are also great brooders and they may care for abandoned eggs. While Cochins are good natured, they are lazy and often overweight because of their low activity level. You should keep them in a fence if you are worried about predators.

One downside is the health issues that come with the breed because of their tendency for obesity. It can be hard to monitor their food intake if you have a variety of breeds. They make good pet chickens, as they are lazier and more relaxed.

Langshan Chickens

Langshan chickens are a good dual-purpose bird. They have large, white meat breasts and are good egg-layers. The Langshan bird is tolerant of all types of climate, excels at foraging, and are good flyers. These chickens are known for their tall stance and large bodies. The Langshan is also a popular choice among breeders because they have been used to create other breeds.

Considering Other Chicken Breeds?

The American Poultry Association has recognized over 60 official breeds of chicken. However, there are hundreds of others that have been created through breeding different birds. The most important thing to do when considering a breed is research. Even though every chicken is unique, it can be incredibly helpful to have insight before you bring a bird home.

Chapter - 5
FEEDING THE CHICKENS

Essentials for Raising Healthy Chickens

Chickens are what they eat. If they are confined to a small environment where they can only eat a limited diet that does not meet their needs, they will suffer and fall ill. For the dedicated chicken keeper, this is something to be avoided at all costs. Apart from the obvious animal cruelty implications, it will also affect the quality of your chickens' meat and create problems with their eggs and chicks. Even a feeding regimen that is lacking in only one essential element can have hugely detrimental effects on your flock.

Diet

A balanced diet for backyard chickens is based on feeding high-quality poultry pellets. These pellets are made up of different quantities of wheat, salt, sunflower seed, maize, and oats. It is presented in an easily digestible format that your chickens will love and will greatly simplify the process of caring for your chickens. As an added bonus, these pellets have balanced quantities of vitamins, nutrients, and minerals that chickens would naturally get from sources such as digested soil, insects, fruits, and vegetables. If your chickens are kept cooped up, this ensures that they don't suffer any dietary deficiencies.

Like any animal, chickens can become bored with a meal, especially if it is all that they are given. One downside of feeding pellets only is that it removes the pleasure of watching your chickens peck and scratch in the dirt. So, it is a good idea to supplement their diets with free grains such as maize (corn) crush or wheat that you can scatter at mealtimes for them to enjoy. You can and should include safe kitchen scraps for them to enjoy as well. These are a great way to boost the vitamin uptake in your chickens, thereby ensuring glossy feathers and limit any illnesses or diseases that your precious flock might develop from malnutrition. Kitchen scraps not only cut down on your feed bill, but it adds another link in sustainable living. As a bonus, your chickens will love you for it!

How Much To Feed

Depending on the size of your chicken, the season, sex of the bird, and their overall health condition, you will need to adjust the feeding quantities of your chickens. In winter, you would feed more, while if you have hens you need to feed more than for roosters. If you have taken on a bird that is underweight you need to gradually increase their feed to avoid them gorging and rupturing their crop where they store food before digesting it in their gizzard. Chickens have a unique digestive system, so overfeeding can be a real problem, especially with young chicks. Smaller sized bits are advisable, and you should take care to feed more regularly in smaller amounts, than a bumper meal once a day. Healthy chickens tend to self-regulate, but when you start, it's a good idea to err on the side of caution.

As a rule of thumb, you can quite safely give a medium-sized handful of pellets per chicken twice a day. An average hen will consume 1.5 pounds of feed per week, so that's a little less than a quarter pound per day. You should keep an eye on your chickens after they have eaten. If they show signs of discomfort or look bloated, it may be an indication that they have been overfed, or that the size of the pellets is too large for them, if it's a smaller breed chicken. Pellets are available in smaller size chunks, which may be better either way.

When feeding, it is a good idea to use several feedings spots or feeding stations as your chickens will have a pecking order. Using only one feeding place will lead to fighting and one or more chickens getting less food than the rest. Always ensure that there is sufficient water available. Chickens prefer drinking at ground level, so avoid high rimmed water feeders. Young chickens can also be clumsy, so don't use buckets of water that they may fall into and drown in.

When your hens are laying eggs, or are brooding on a clutch of eggs, it may be necessary for you to provide a special feed that is balanced to help them make up the calcium and protein loss that goes into the eggs. For hens brooding on their eggs, they will be spending approximately 21 days and will only rarely venture from their eggs. It may be kind to place a small amount of feed and water near the nest, to help her keep up her body weight and stay fed.

What to Feed or Not Feed

Apart from the balanced chicken feed pellets, you are encouraged to supplement your chickens' diet with scraps and treats. You may be concerned with what can be safely fed to your chickens, and what will improve their health. Always bear in mind that chickens are omnivores, and they will eat sometimes questionable foods that may not be good for their health, if not toxic. Some flowers are quite toxic to chickens, so it's a better idea to avoid feeding flowers. You could instead feed vegetable scraps, which are more nutritious and less harmful to your birds. It may be a little upsetting the first time that your chickens devour a juicy burger from McDonald's with gusto. Cannibalism is quite prevalent among chickens, and they will happily gobble up bones, which are a rich source of calcium. To avoid future problems, it may be a better idea to let them peck at calcium sources such as oyster shells to avoid them turning on their own flock members. Ground-up eggshells are a good source of calcium, but to avoid them pecking at their own eggs, it is a wise practice to mash the eggs up so that they don't "identify" the shells as being eggs.

In some countries and states, it is illegal to feed certain scraps to chickens since these can spread diseases. Caution should be taken when feeding anything that is of an animal nature, so even though chickens will devour beef, poultry, sheep, pork, and fish, it is better to avoid these. Organically grown mealworms suitable for feeding to chickens can be ordered online, though other types are still illegal due to these worms being raised on animal proteins that could transfer diseases to your flock. A few juicy mealworms as a treat around molting time make for a great protein boost for your hens. However, free-ranging birds will happily chase down their own sources of proteins from spiders and moths to worms and crickets. They love eating plant lice as well and will help keep your garden louse free.

Vegetable kitchen scraps can be fed, if it is low in salts and sugars, which are bad for chickens. However, you should take care to only feed fresh scraps and remove whatever the chickens don't finish to avoid attracting flies. Leftover foods can also form mold, which is bad for your chickens and can lead to salmonella poisoning.

These vegetables, fruits, grains, and animal proteins are safe for chickens.

Broccoli: High in vitamins, can be given cooked.

Tomatoes: Although a fruit, it is also considered a vegetable. Chickens love the tomato itself, but you should never give them the leaves or plant as this is highly toxic to chickens. The fruit is rich in vitamin C, K & B9 and also antioxidants.

Potatoes: You can give chickens raw or cooked potatoes or sweet potatoes, but not any sections that are green as this contains solanine, which is toxic. Never give them the leaves, stems, or flowers of the potato plant.

Cabbage: A big yes on this. It is loaded with trace minerals and vitamins that your chickens will love. As a bonus, you could hang the head of cabbage or place it in a wire cage that your chickens could play with to relieve boredom if they are cooped up.

Popcorn: A bit of a no-brainer, since popcorn is corn, which chickens love. Just ensure that there is no sugar, salt, or butter on. It is high in vitamins A, E & K. Your flock will love playing with the popped kernels.

Bananas: A lovely treat for hens as it's rich in vitamins B6, C & A and contains iron and magnesium to help with their general health. Again, you could tie up a few banana peels like little treasures along the chicken run to keep your chickens busy. Avoid feeding them green bananas though.

Apples: Chickens love apples due to the sweet taste. Any fruit should be given in moderation due to the rich sugar content. Fruit seeds are also indigestible to chickens and may be slightly toxic to them, so remove any seeds before feeding.

Cut grass: Your chickens will naturally peck away at your lawn if they have access. However, if they are in a coop or chicken run without access, you can supplement them by adding a few handfuls of untreated cut grass to their diet every other day. Make sure that the cuttings are fine to avoid their crops becoming tied up. The small seeds that grass forms in summer are a real treat to chickens.

Rice: Brown rice is best and rich in nutrients, however with any whole grain you should cook it before sharing with your chickens. Raw grains will soak up moisture in the chickens' digestive tracts and expand causing indigestion and even death. This is another reason why you should avoid feeding bread to young chickens. Traditionally, bread is fed to hens before slaughtering to fatten them up, but it can cause your chickens to tie up and die.

Crickets: You can purchase crickets online or from pet stores, and these are wonderful treats to brooding hens. At 12.9 grams of protein and 5.5 grams per 100 grams serving, they can help a chicken that is underweighted to perk up quickly. You may need to feed this in moderation though to avoid getting overweight chickens, unless you plan on slaughtering them.

Berries: Chickens will love eating berries, but be careful considering the high sugar content, and the unexpected change in color of their droppings. Berries are rich in vitamins and antioxidants.

Pumpkin: This is an excellent nutritious source that is also entertaining for chickens. You could place a halved pumpkin (preferably a well-matured orange or yellow one) in their coop to keep them busy for several days. The seeds are also great at keeping your flock naturally worm-free.

Carrots: A big yes on this. If you have young chicks, you may need to rough dice this for them. Generally, chickens love carrots and will happily enjoy the foliage part too. It's a rich source of vitamins and minerals.

Oats: Raw or cooked oats are a stimulating treat for your chickens. Pullets also seem to respond well to it with a reduction in habits such as feather pecking. In winter, it is a great way to help warm up your flock by giving small amounts of warmed oatmeal to them. It should not be given too frequently though as the processed forms of oats that we buy from the shop tend to be slightly congestive to the chicken crop.

Cauliflower stems: Chickens love this, and it is a nutritious snack. They aren't really interested in the heads though.

Salads: You can feed most leftover scraps of salads, however, remember that it has likely been seasoned with salts that are bad for your chickens. It would be better to feed scraps before adding spices and salts to your salads. Chickens love pecking at lettuce and even cucumber pieces. Peppers tend to not be a favorite among chickens, and the plants are toxic, so avoid it.

Chapter - 6
TYPES OF ALIMENTATION

Once you have decided on your breed of chicken and built a coop then you need to understand how to feed and water your chickens. This is very important because a well looked after chicken is going to produce you a lot more eggs than one which is not happy.

Chickens like fresh, growing grass such as buckwheat or clover and eat all types of broadleaf weeds including both the seeds and the growing tips. They also like slugs, insects and worms, being happy to roam between your vegetable plants picking up the slugs. They also need grit to help them digest their food. Chickens will also occasionally catch small rodents too.

You can feed your chickens the scraps left off from your kitchen; though don't feed them potatoes because raw potatoes can be poisonous to chickens. You should avoid feeding your chickens garlic, onions and beans because it can influence that flavor of the eggs.

Chickens also aren't particularly bright, and they will eat almost anything, so you need to keep an eye on them. They will eat Styrofoam and they will even, from time to time, eat the pine shavings that are used as their litter!

Not everyone is able to give their chickens a pasture to run in, but you can at least give them a run where they can supplement their diet with the occasional insect. If you do pasture your chickens, then you need to make sure that you protect them from predators.

You can supplement their diet with oyster shells, which gives your chickens calcium. If you want to give them something to entertain them then give them a cabbage head as they will love that.

If you run out of chicken feed you can feed them with kitchen scraps and they can go a day or two without feed, but no longer.

There are a wide range of different commercial feeds on the market that you can choose on and some are specific to a certain species or a certain age chicken. Check the feed that you are feeding your chickens and see if you need to change their feed when they hit a certain age.

Types of Feed

Pellets: This is feed that is made into pellet form for easy use.

Crumbles: These are pellets that are broken into chick-size pieces to make it easy to eat.

Mash: Unprocessed chicken feed that is almost powder-like

Fermented: Any type of chicken feed mixed with water and allowed to naturally ferment.

Medicated: This feed is treated with coccidiostat to help chickens defeat any attack from coccidian protozoa, which comes from them eating food or water contaminated with infected soil or poop from infected birds. Don't use this feed if your chickens have been vaccinated.

What's in Chicken Feed?

Back in the 1900s, chickens would have to survive on table scraps and whatever they could find. Scientific research has come a long way since then, and we now know that all chicken feed should contain:

Protein. The amount of protein varies based on the bird age or type of bird. For example, if you're raising a bird to eat, they will require a high protein content.

Amino Acids.

Vitamins and Minerals. Usually, vitamins A, E, D3 and B12 are added, as well as trace minerals like phosphorus and copper sulfate.

Enzymes. These help with digestion.

Fiber. This comes from the grain in the feed

Other additives. You've seen commercials about Omega 3 eggs. Some feeds have Omega 3 added, which increases the amount in the eggs, making them healthier to eat.

Chickens need about 20 grams of protein a day to produce an egg.

Be sure to read all product labels so you know what's in your feed.

When your pullets (female chickens) begin laying eggs, feed them layer feed. This feed has 16 percent protein and doesn't have as many vitamins as feed for meat chickens or chicks. If you start with one feed and change feeds, be sure to do it slowly, because a quick change can cause diarrhea or other stomach issues. This doesn't apply to the type of feed; if you start with crumbles, you can change to pellets of the same brand with no problems.

Fermented feed is healthier for your birds, and if you have a small flock, it's easy to make. In soaking the feed and grains, locked-in nutrients are released. You'll also use less feed, so it's a great way to lower your feed bill.

The Natural Chicken Water

Chickens also need clean drinking water, and a regular supply of it. There are a lot of things to consider, including how you are going to get the water to them and ensure that it doesn't freeze over in winter. You should never restrict or limit your chicken's access to water as without it they will not lay particularly well, and their growth will be hampered.

As a rough guide, each adult laying hen will drink around one pint of water each day. This can vary according to the size of the chicken and the temperature. In hotter weather they drink a quart of water a day. Meat birds usually require even more water because it helps them to grow faster.

Your chickens will not like dirty water or water that is too warm. You may also add vitamins to their water and that could stop them drinking it, they can be quite fussy! Scrub their water bowl out regularly and ensure that it is clean. You are going to need to change their water daily to ensure that they keep drinking it.

There are a few different types if chicken waterer, including automatic systems that provide fresh water constantly to your chickens. Which you choose will depend upon the number of chickens you have, your budget and a few other factors.

The most commonly used waterer is the round one. This is made of plastic or metal and it has a trough at the bottom with a shallow lip which is where the chickens drink from. It works on a vacuum system which ensures the lip is constantly filled with water.

These are the most popular waterers and they work very well. It is better if you raise them up of the ground either by hanging them from the roof of the coop or putting them on a stand. This stops litter shavings and chicken poop ended up in the water, which will stop them from drinking it.

You can get open bowls, but these don't tend to work very well because the chickens have a tendency to walk through them and knock them over. With open bowls your chickens are going to get filthy and soaking wet pretty quickly.

It is possible for you to make a chicken waterer. You will need a five-gallon bucket as well as a shallow plastic dish. You drill some small holes in the side of your bucket lower than the top of the plate's lip. You then need to seal the bucket and the plate together with an airtight seal. You want to ensure that this seal is airtight so that the vacuum pressure will stop the water leaking out of the bucket all at once. You can weld it if everything is made out of metal or you can use a combination of superglues and waterproof sealant.

There are nipple systems which you can buy and attach to the bottom of a five-gallon bucket to create a gravity fed system for delivering water to your chickens. You do need to ensure the nipples dot get clogged by lime in the water or dirt though. However, it's a great system for a beginner as it is very easy to use and affordable,

There are a number of different automatic waterers on the market and the dog bowl style waterer which you can connect to a garden hose. You can get the industrial automatic chicken waterers though these aren't really cost effective unless you have a large number of chickens.

You need to make sure that the water doesn't freeze in winter because then the chickens can't drink when they want to. You will either need to give them fresh water twice a day or you can get heated waterers which ensure the water doesn't freeze over. If you live in a cold climate where it freezes regularly then it is worth investing in a heated waterer to ensure your chickens have access to water in the colder months.

Once you have all of these items you are ready to keep chickens. As you can see, they don't need a lot of things but you do need to ensure you get the right items for both your climate and the type of chickens you are planning on keeping.

Feeders

There are many types of feeders, and you can keep them outside in the run, or in your coop, if it is large enough. Keep in mind that when your chickens roost at night, they sleep and won't get up to eat or drink. But, it's all-too easy for predators to get to food when it's left outside.

Metal or Plastic? Metal feeders are harder to find, but they often outlast plastic feeders; sun and snow are hard on plastic.

Automatic/Treadle Feeders: This is a great option if you have to work late or travel. The hens have to learn to stand on the platform in order for the feed box to open. Chickens are smart. They'll learn fast. But raccoons are smart, too, so if you have a feeder like this and leave it outside, be sure you have a way to lock it.

Hanging Feeders: These are also

known as "gravity feeders," because that's how they work. It's a large bucket with a ring underneath that holds the food. Per the Happy Chicken Coop, these are hands-down the best-selling type of feeder, whether they hang, or are mounted on a wall or in a corner. Have a couple of these in your coop so the chickens don't all crowd at once. And, there are some bully hens who will guard a feeder as her property, which means no one else gets to eat. So, have more than one. If you plan to feed outside, some come with rain guards to prevent food from getting wet.

Trough Feeders: This type of feeder is especially popular for small chicks, but one of the best things about this style is that many hens can fit around the feeder at the same time. Make sure if you buy this type of feeder that it comes with legs to keep it above the ground. And, an advantage of this feeder is that chickens don't sit in it, so they can't poop in it. Also be sure to get a modern tube-and-trough gravity feeder to keep the feed from getting dirty.

Pest Proof: Look for this kind of feeder if you're having a problem with things like rats or mice.

Chick Feeders: These are smaller versions of adult feeders. Many of them have round bases so you can fill a Mason jar with feed and screw it into the base.

Chapter - 7
CARE AND CHICKEN MAINTENANCE

Young chicks are very delicate to handle. They require lots of care and constant attention. So, if you choose to raise hens from day old chicks, you need to make sure that you have no time-consuming engagements, or some family member is there for them

The first thing is assembling all the supplies you need for these chicks well in advance before you bring them forth, you'll require a brooder, heat lamp, feeder and waterer. You also need to designate an area where they'll first stay before they can move into the coop. Generally, chicks require just a little space since they are already small and will be moving to the coop in about four weeks. A garage, workshop, or a specially made coop will do fine. You just need to make sure that the chosen area is predator proof, weatherproof and easily accessible at all times. The chosen area should also be safe from scary noises that might make the chicks frightened. They can easily die of fright. If you choose a room with a cement floor, find some cardboard and enclose them to limit their movements. Take note not to create corners as they tend to hurdle around corners and smother each other to death. A cardboard box with some high walls might be sufficient if you just have a few chicks. You will have to cover the floor with some form of bedding. Wood shavings, sawdust, dried up leaves will be good choices. However, since the chicks will have very small and weak legs, you can cover these with a paper towel for the first week. Their legs can easily go different directions in an even surface and break. If this happens there's no cure. If you already had an area where you had previous chicks, it will be important to disinfect to kill any lingering germs. Chicks have weak immune systems that can get easily compromised.

Chicks will need a constant supply of heat that they would normally get from their mother. You need a heat lamp to provide this heat. Test your heat lamp before you bring in the chicks. You should have two for security. if you just have one and it malfunction, your chicks might not survive. A 250 watts infrared heat lamp is recommended since it's not very bright and will provide the required heat. During the first week, they'll need 95 degrees which you will reduce by 5 degrees for each subsequent week. The heat lamp should be suspended right to the area where the chicks will be staying. The suspension mechanism should lower or rise if you need to control the heat. If the chicks are scrambling together, it means they are feeling cold and you need to lower the heat lamp to increase the temperature. If they are going further from the heat source and look restless, raise the heat lamp higher to reduce the temperatures. An adverse temperature can kill them within hours. That is why we talked about constant attention.

The paper towels that will serve as bedding will only be good for the first week. Small chicks poop big, since they are constantly feeding. The towels won't keep up with this. By the second week the legs will be strong enough to withstand most types of bedding. You need to make sure that you keep on changing the bedding to make them comfortable and keep them dry.

The chicks will be feeding right from the first day they get to your home. They have enough stock to last them three days from the yolk, but they nibble on anything they find even during this time. Provide water and food right from the word go. It's helpful to treat their water with some nutrients to strengthen them. A tablespoon of molasses to 4 liters of water will be good for them. A tablespoon of vinegar/apple cider vinegar added to the water will also be good for their immune system. However, if you notice any blood in their poop, you'll need to use a tablespoon of vinegar for every liter of water. The water container should be something small and shallow. You don't have to purchase one; you could easily convert a plate for this purpose. Make sure to change the water every so often. Same for feed, find some container which will be easily accessible to them. You have to start them on commercial feeds right away. Choose the starter feeds which will make them start their development with the needed nutrients.

Small chicks will often be affected by what's normally known as pasty butt. This is the blocking of their vent opening by their caked-up droppings. You will need to keep an eye out for this right from taking them out of the box they came in. If not cleared up, this condition will kill them. When you notice it, use a wet cloth or paper towel to gently unblock them. You could also use the paper towel and a toothpick. If it's really blocked, you have no choice but to dip the chicks' backside into warm water for a short time. Coccidiosis is another common condition which will be present if the chicks are unvaccinated. Medicated feeds from the start will prevent it and if it does occur, a tablespoon of vinegar for every liter of water will save the non-infected chicks.

Chapter - 8
DISEASES

These are the most common problems that backyard keepers are likely to see in their flock at some point.

Bumblefoot

We mentioned this earlier in our health check list. Bumblefoot is caused by the bacteria Staph. Aureus. Its' point of entry is usually a miniscule cut to the foot pad or a splinter. The wound will heal, but a 'bumble' will grow. It is a black, usually circular patch of skin which can be on the foot pad or between the toes. When noticed early it can be treated with antibiotics, occasionally it may need to be surgically removed. If left untreated, it can cause system wide infection from which the hen will die.

Vent Prolapse

This is an emergency! It arises from one of the following:

· Too large an egg which makes the hen strain to expel it

- Young pullets made to lay too soon

- Older, fat hens

- Calcium deficiency

The good news is it is treatable, but the bad news is it is likely to happen again. Prolapsed vent is quite easy to spot, the vent turns itself inside out so there is a red, glistening protrusion at the back end. You will need to isolate this hen immediately since her sisters will peck at it causing further damage. You will need to clean all the tissue well with a mild antiseptic solution or plain soap and warm water. Apply a hemorrhoid cream to the vent inside and out, then with your gloved finger, gently insert the vent back into the hen. It may pop out a couple of times but keep on re-inserting using the above sequence each time.

The hen needs to stay quiet for a few days, so put her in a dimly lit area to discourage her from laying. She will need to be given extra vitamin, calcium and electrolytes in her water. Once she has healed, you can re-introduce her to the flock slowly. Keep a close watch on her, as prolapsed vent has a tendency to reoccur.

Egg Yolk Peritonitis

Egg yolk peritonitis happens when the yolk is released from the ovary into the body cavity instead of the infundibulum (oviduct). The yolk is an almost perfect medium for bacteria to set up shop in. The bacteria in question can be E. Coli, salmonella or pasteurella. As we already mentioned, hens are very good at hiding the fact they are ill, so by the time you have usually noted the symptoms the hen is extremely ill. Symptoms include pale comb/wattles; dull eyes; reluctant to move; sitting alone; looks disheveled and swollen abdomen. If your hen exhibits any of these symptoms, she should be taken to the vet as soon as possible, peritonitis is an emergency. The treatment is antibiotics, but unfortunately this problem has a very high mortality rate.

Egg Bound

If your hen is walking like a penguin or you are seeing her pumping her tail up and down, she is trying to expel an egg. To confirm your suspicions, you can gently insert your gloved and lubed index finger into her vent. You need to go straight back for about one to two inches very gently. You may be able to feel the egg, if you do apply more lubrication inside the vent. Then soak her abdomen in warm water and Epsom salts for twenty minutes or so, gently massaging her belly at the same time. Remove her from the tub, gently towel her off and apply a hemorrhoidal cream to the vent area. Place her in a quiet, darkened safe place and check on her in an hour to see if she has passed the egg. If she hasn't try the soaking tub again, you may need to repeat this a few times. If after three times she doesn't pass the egg, she will need taking to the local veterinarian.

Marek's Disease

Marek's disease is caused by a herpes virus and is quite widespread over the continent. It will depend on the particular strain that your bird may catch as to presentation of symptoms. The severity of the virus can be non-apparent (no symptoms) to the disturbing sight of the neurological presentation. In its most dramatic presentation, the bird will seemingly do the splits, be unable to weight bear, its head may twist back, and it will suffer severe respiratory distress. There is no cure for Marek's disease yet. The vaccine does not confer immunity; it will only make the symptoms lessen in severity.

Marek's has a few different presentations, one of which is the internal growth of tumors. These tumors are only noticed postmortem. Many flocks are infected with Marek's and yet show no symptoms at all and the birds live out their life in full. Marek's disease should not be seen as a 'death sentence' to your flock, as some flock members may succumb to it while others will not be affected. The survivors will be carriers for the rest of their days.

Frostbite

Frostbite occurs when damp cold air freezes the extremities of an animal. In chickens it is usually the comb, wattles and feet. This is one reason that good ventilation is essential in the coop. Chickens can tolerate cold much better than humans as they have lots of feathers to keep them warm. When there is moisture in the air, it will form condensation on exposed surfaces. Roosters are always prime candidates for frozen combs and wattles, as are breeds with large combs such as Leghorns.

Preventative measures include adequate ventilation, reduction of drafts blowing on the birds, placing wider perches so they can cover their feet with the feathers and using Vaseline or similar on combs and wattles to form a barrier between the air and skin.

Chapter - 9
BEHAVIOR AND CHICKEN PSYCHOLOGY

PECKING ORDER

There is no such thing as democracy or equality in a flock. Chickens maintain social order through authoritarian rule. Their social hierarchy is called the pecking order, because they literally peck one another into submission.

Pecking order is actually a very complex social structure with lots of nuances. In a mixed flock, there are three distinct types of interactions and subhierarchies: hen to hen, rooster to hen, and rooster to rooster.

The subhierarchies really complicate the social rules, but somehow the chickens still manage to exist in relative harmony.

The alpha hen is flock queen. Her status affords her priority access to all the best spots in the coop and yard. Her subordinates will always yield, so that she will get the most preferred nest, the best dust-bathing hole, the best shady napping space, a favorite roosting spot, and whatever she deems is rightfully hers. The second highest ranking hen (the beta) will get second choice, and so forth down the line.

If a lower-ranking hen doesn't yield or is slow to move out of the way for a higher-ranking member, she may receive a quick but fierce stare, like one of those "You better not!" mom looks. The subordinate may also get a peck on the head, and that may even be followed by a chest bump or other acts of dominance.

The queen's role isn't all about privilege, though. The general well-being and harmony of the flock weighs heavily on her wings. Because she's a strong, healthy leader, she must protect and maintain order in the flock.

It's the queen's job to warn against dangerous threats and to guide the flock to safety. Furthermore, while she has the right, a good queen actually doesn't eat first very often. Instead, she will allow her subjects to eat while she guards the flock from predators. When they're done eating, or when her beta or appointed sentry is available to help keep watch, the queen will then eat.

The higher-ranking hens often also serve as judges, mediators, and peacekeepers whenever there is discord. If a fight or squabble between some flock members goes on too long, the queen, the sentry, or another high-ranking hen will intervene and break up the fight. The mediator-judge will insert herself between the squabblers and issue a couple of pecks. She also may jump-kick and flog the squabbler she judges to be more at fault.

Sometimes a hen (or junior rooster) will take the role of sentry. Her role may vary a little, depending on flock size and dynamics. We had a sentry that took her job very seriously, but she was not high on the pecking order, as you might assume. She was somewhere in the middle. She patrolled the food area during mealtime and was always first to attempt to break up a fight. At dusk, she stood guard in front of the coop door, waiting for each flock member to come home, as if she was conducting a census. She would harass younger birds, who she didn't consider full-fledged members of the flock, and attempt to block their entry.

If there is a rooster in the flock, he usually is alpha—the flock king. He takes on all the burdens and responsibilities of the queen in an all-hen flock. He guards, finds food, and ensures the flock's overall safety and harmony. There will still be a flock queen, and she still has all the privileges, but just slightly less responsibility.

If there's more than one rooster, the roosters will rank themselves in a descending hierarchy and assign privileges and rules according to position. This ranking is separate from their overall flock ranking.

CHICKEN CALLS

Early research has found that chickens are able to make at least 24 distinct chicken sounds. The sounds used together and in combination with movements, such as a head tilt, a look, a wing flap, or a run, can communicate a lot of things, like "Hawk! Defcon 2!" "Squirrel alert!" or "Hey, I found a lizard!"

With recording technology and artificial intelligence software, researchers have been able to predict and detect whether chickens are happy, stressed, or ill based on the sounds, tone, and volume of their vocalizations. You and I won't have AI to help us decipher chicken talk, but with some listening and observation, you can still learn chickenese.

BABY TALK

The cute, happy sounds we associate with chicks are sounds of contentment. When they're particularly happy during nap or snuggle time, they will trill, which is basically a chicken purr.

Their sounds of displeasure are sharp and loud. You'll hear the startled sound when you accidentally sneak up on them. They vocalize a cry indicating fear when you reach into the brooder to pick them up before they've gotten used to you. When they're too hot, too cold, or hungry, they make sounds of distress. When they're lost or can't see their buddies, they make a very loud panicked call to their mates.

MAMA CALLS

Mama hens will have some distinct calls and sounds when they're instructing their chicks to follow closely, when they've found some food, when they're warning the chicks of potential dangers, and when they're instructing them to stay hidden. Mama hens will also cluck and chat with their chicks while the babies are inside the eggs—and the chicks chirp back!

ANGRY BIRDS

If you disturb a hen while she's laying or when she's broody, you'll certainly experience her wrath. When a hen "goes broody," her hormones tell her that she needs to sit on and hatch some eggs. Disturbing a laying or broody hen will result in a very angry scream: "GO AWAY!!!!!" and some other colorful cackles. The hen may also hiss, growl, and puff herself up to look more menacing.

At night, some birds will growl, whine, and grumble when they don't want another hen roosting near them. They'll peck the other hens while telling them to scram. The pecked hens will vocalize fear and virtually say "Ow!"

When you handle a hen, who doesn't want to be picked up, she'll sure cackle something like "Let me go! Helllllp!"

CHICKCHAT

The flock will communicate with one another throughout the day, like when they're following one another to a great feeding or dusting spot, as if to say, "This is a good spot!" or "Let's go this way." Sometimes they just look and sound like they're catching up on the latest gossip.

When going into the yard, my chickens walk toward me and cluck various greetings. If they get really excited or think I have some treats, some will fly off our back hill while making loud cackles, as if to say, "Hi! Wait for me! I'm coming!" I don't know if the cackles are directed to me, to the flock, or maybe both.

Beluga, a quirky, attention-seeking hen, will growl at others to stay away from me, while making demanding squawks and whines instructing me to pet and cuddle her. If I don't oblige, she will complain and scrape and peck me with her beak until I do. Or she'll take matters into her own wings and fly onto my back or head. Once cuddled, she makes soft, low sounds and purrs of contentment mixed with warning grumbles to other chickens who come too close. Some hens make a squeakier string of clucks when you cuddle them, as if to say, "Aww, this feels nice."

SOUND THE ALARM!

Chickens have a number of sounds for danger, and there are differences in sound for an aerial predator versus a ground predator. The length, tone, and pitch of an alarm call indicates the threat level. Some mean "Careful!" while others mean "Incoming! Ruuuuunnnnn!"

ROOSTER DYNAMICS

If your city happens to allow a rooster, you're in for a treat if you keep one. In my case, we didn't initially intend on keeping a rooster, but my drama queen chick Cher turned out to be RuPaul.

Having a rooster creates a new and interesting flock dynamic. A good flock king is assertive, confident, and responsible. Some hens will be quite enamored and follow him closely. Some will remain unimpressed and want nothing to do with him. He will have a favorite hen, too. When she falls out of favor, it's interesting to watch their dynamics change. He'll even move his nightly roosting spot to be next to the new favorite. It's like a juicy soap opera.

Roosters often engage in a behavior called tidbitting. A rooster will repeatedly pick up and drop food, while rapidly calling guk-guk-guk-guhk-guhk, and his comb and wattles will wobble with movement. It's all designed to attract hens. When they come, he may drop a wing and circle a hen in a little mating dance. Tidbitting is part of mating behavior, whether or not he engages in dance, because being a gentleroo (my term for being gentlemanly, generous, and courteous) does impress the hens—and sometimes you too! RuPaul tidbits and dances for me frequently.

tidbitting mating behavior of a rooster, characterized by repeated vocalizations (a food call) while picking up and dropping a bit of food

Most roosters will always yield and let their hens have all the tastiest treats first—although I've had some with not-so-good gentleroo behavior. They'll look around slyly to see if anyone is around, then selfishly taking all the treats for themselves.

Roosters can be deceptive, too. Sometimes they'll tidbit with a stick to trick a hen who is farther away to come closer, thus increasing their chances of mating. They may also fake tidbit to trick a rival (like another rooster) to come closer before attacking. RuPaul views toddlers as his rivals and will fake tidbit when he sees them.

Maintaining good flock harmony and security is an important duty. The rooster mediates and breaks up any henpecking or fights, protects weaker hens, and helps prevent bullying in general. Whether the flock is dust bathing, foraging, lounging, or eating, he stands guard nearby and alerts them of dangers. If necessary, a rooster will defend the flock and fight a predator.

Roosters engage in nesting behaviors, too. When a near-laying pullet is looking for a nest, he'll lead her to the nest boxes, rearrange the bedding, and call her in to inspect his work. He'll continue until she's satisfied and selects a laying spot.

My flock's king, Uno (RuPaul's son), always selflessly gives his treats to his hens. He never secretly gobbles down a treat, and he's always the last to eat, because duty comes first. If I'm slow to feed and the flock is hungry, he'll crow incessantly to let me know, and will run up to complain when I appear. When the chickens forage on the hilly part of our yard, he positions himself in a good lookout spot near his hens to watch for predators. Uno is also very gentle with people, and even children.

BAD BEHAVIOR: EGG EATING

A happy flock has few behavior problems. Behavior problems generally indicate discord and discontent within the flock. There are several simple things you can do to correct any behavior problems. First and foremost, prevention is key. Make sure you start off right with the information and tips I've provided throughout this manuscript. Observe and check regularly to make sure your flock is happy.

EGG EATING

Egg eating usually occurs for the same reasons as bullying—stress, overcrowding, boredom, food issues. Other reasons could be not having enough nest boxes, inexperienced hens, or too much light in the nest boxes.

Chickens naturally are curious and explore their environment with their beak. If they're stressed, their anxiety manifests in pecking. An accidental broken egg can trigger the start of this bad habit. Once they have a taste, and maybe in combination with one or more of the risk factors I just mentioned, egg eating can be the result.

Chapter - 10
EGGS

When do hens start laying eggs?

Pullets will come into lay at about 6 months of age. Breed will play a role in when this happens as will whether you have a rooster or not. Roosters can encourage young hens to start laying sooner, but that is not always the case. As your hens start laying, try and keep track of which hen is laying what eggs. Having a mixed breed flock makes this easier. Keeping track of who is laying what and when will help you identify any issues that may arise.

As hens begin laying, the consistency will be low and they may even begin laying, stop, and start again a few times. New laying hens may also lay what are commonly known as fairy eggs. These are just tiny little eggs that get laid by a hen that did not ovulate fully. Usually fairy eggs are just a small amount of albumen surrounded by a shell and usually lack a yolk or have a very small yolk.

I discard fairy eggs; they are common and normal, nothing to worry about. Your hens will also start to understand how to lay in the nesting boxes. You will probably find their first eggs in a random place and the eggs will probably be dirty. New hens get better at leaving them clean and in the right spot, especially if you leave out dummy eggs or golf balls in the nesting boxes where you want them to lay.

Egg Collection

Once your hens start laying, you will want to collect the eggs often. Twice a day is recommended but be sure to collect at least once a day. If you are only going to collect once, get them in the afternoon after all the hens have laid. If you check often at first, you will notice certain hens lay their eggs consistently at the same time and can adjust when you collect accordingly.

Leaving eggs in nesting boxes overnight or longer is a bad idea for a few reasons. It attracts predators and the eggs are more likely to get broken, resulting in egg eating hens. It is also hard to keep track of when certain eggs were laid and that can result in a finding bad egg.

Cleaning Eggs

After you have collected your eggs, examine them for cracks. You will want to discard cracked eggs because there is a higher chance, they have bacteria in them. You can scramble them up and feed them back to your chickens, throw them away, or throw them in your compost bin – just be sure they brake so you do not end up with a rotten egg!

The good eggs may need a little cleaning, mine rarely do. When an egg is laid, it has a special layer called a "bloom" on the shell that protects the egg. Eggshells are porous and once wet; the bloom is gone which means they can potentially absorb any liquid that sits on them for long periods of time. For this reason, there is great debate on whether you should wash eggs or not. Always brush off any dirt or poop with a rough cloth or pad. If you have good nesting boxes, the eggs should not have much debris on them.

If you do choose to wash your eggs, do not use anything but very warm water and a mild soap like dish soap (be sure to rinse briefly after the soap) and do not soak the eggs. Dry the eggs immediately and always store washed eggs or eggs that became wet in the fridge.

Unwashed eggs with the bloom still intact can be kept at room temperature but they will go bad more quickly. The whole reason we keep food in the fridge is to keep it fresh for a longer amount of time. Try and keep track of the eggs that are oldest and use those first, but eggs will last quite a while in your fridge.

I need room temperature eggs for many things I bake, so I keep some on the counter and some in the fridge. I have never had issues either way.

Problems with Eggs

There are many issues that can arise in the laying flock. Almost all of them can be tied back to inappropriate nutrition or failure to deworm your hens. This means that proper feeding and deworming can avoid most issues, which is good news! Those are easy fixes. You can also have egg problems when there is stress or sickness in your flock, but often a stressed or sick bird will totally stop laying. The most common issues are calcium deposits on your eggs, soft shells, and deformed eggs.

Egg Binding

Having a hen that is egg bound means she has an egg stuck in her vent. This will become life threatening to your hen, so you should take the necessary steps to try and help her. Here is what you can try first:

Separate the hen from the flock.

Soak her body in warm water.

Lubricate the egg being careful not to break it and gently massage the abdomen of the hen.

Leave her in a dark room alone to see if it will pass on it's own.

If these steps do not relieve your hen, you may need to try and remove the egg yourself. If possible, have a veterinarian help you at this point. If you do not have access to a veterinarian, the best way to remove the egg is to aspirate the contents with a syringe and then gently remove the shell.

Even if you just have one hen that is having egg issues, you are going to need to re-evaluate your nutrition and housing situation to make sure it is appropriate. Most likely it will be a nutrition issue or a deworming issue.

How Age Effects Laying

The age of a laying hen is directly related to how often she will lay and what her eggs will be like. Here is how you can expect age to impact your flock:

Irregular production

Smaller eggs.

Pullets, up to 1 year old.

Still learning how and when and where to lay eggs.

Peak production

"Normal" sized eggs.

2-3 years and older.

Decreasing production

Eggs get larger with age.

Increased risk for egg issues and health problems.

Older than 3-4 years.

Stop laying

Mobility issues.

Increased frailty.

Decreased cold hardiness.

Options for Old Hens

What should you do with older hens in your flock? There are a few options.

Keep them: You can always keep old hens and allow them to live out their days in your flock.

Sell them: Some people like to keep chickens as pets and would love a friendly older hen.

Harvest them: If it does not bother you, you can always use them for meat. They will probably be very tough and only make good soup though.

It is important to note that there is no right or wrong answer here. It is a personal choice and up to you. Choose the option that is the best fit for your flock and do not feel guilty about what you end up choosing.

Chapter - 11
CHICKEN LAWS

Raising chickens might be subject to a variety of laws and regulations, depending on where you live or where you plan to build your coop. Before getting started with the whole business of raising chickens in your backyard, find out if there are nay local ordinances or restrictions that might cause potential problems in the future.

The first thing is to find out what jurisdiction covers the place where you are in as well as the municipality, township, or parish. You can contact people from the local government regarding laws and ordinances in your town or city that may affect agricultural or poultry ventures. There is usually an information desk one can inquire at, to find out the right authority able to tell you about what you need. If they have online resources such as a website or webpage, it is also a good idea to look into them. If all of that searching becomes futile, or if no one is sure about legislature regarding livestock, then you can make inquiries from the local animal control officer. A visit to the local courthouse may also be helpful in finding out about local laws in your city or town.

There are such things as subdivision covenants that you might encounter, depending on the place your property is situated in. They are not formal laws that are enforced by the local government so the association that the covenant is connected to might seek help from a lawyer to go after you, in case of any violations. On the other hand, the association may have already gone inactive so there would be no one left to enforce the said covenant.

What to Expect

Permits and or fees: Before you can set up a chicken coop, some localities might require the payment of a small fee or acquirement of a permit. For others, a permit is only required if the number of birds you have exceeds that of the amount set within the local law.

Number of animals permitted per household: As was mentioned above, some localities might require a set number of birds that you are allowed to have. This is primarily due to the limits in spacing. The size of the property or lot is often taken into consideration when deciding this specific number. The most common number set would be probably about three to four. Fines may be imposed if you exceed a particular number or a permit may be required if you want to own more than the set amount.

Regulation for roosters: The main cause for concern when raising roosters is the noise and disturbances that they might cause. There are places that allow keeping of roosters and there are places that don't. Some allow them as long as the rooster is below four months of age. Since the main reason of keeping chickens are for the eggs they yield, it is generally acceptable to keep and raise only hens

Space requirements: Some localities have a set of requirements for the size of the enclosure or chicken coop. Most especially in urban and suburban areas, free ranging is generally disallowed. Not all places however have this specific requirement. It is best to ask local authorities for clearer instructions.

Nuisance Clauses: These clauses vary from place to place but the statements included usually relate to excessive noise; offensive smells; attraction of flies, rodents, and other pests; cleanliness and waste disposal issues; and public health and infection concerns.

Restrictions on animal slaughtering: Another benefit of raising chickens is the possible yield of edible meat. In some places, the regulations regarding slaughtering of chickens in residential areas are unclear but most do put some sort of a restriction on it. Other places permit slaughtering and still other only allow it within the confines of a building to avoid conflicts with neighboring residents.

Distance restrictions: Some localities specify restrictions on the distance of the chicken coop from neighboring property lines or nearby residences. Again, some have restrictions, some don't, and others are unclear. The distance restrictions from property lines are less common than distance requirements regarding residences. Distances between property lines range from ten to ninety feet while distance restrictions from coops to residences are about twenty to fifty feet.

Other regulations: There are common laws and regulations but there are also those that are unique to a specific town or city. Some examples are:

Storage of the chicken feed or food in specific containers

An additional chicken may be owned and added to the set of allowable number of chickens for every square feet of property owned

Chickens may be only allowed in specific areas or zones

Changing Laws

If the laws where you live are a bit too restrictive, it is possible to bring about some changes. There are documented instances where individuals have been successful at changing their local laws or ordinances regarding backyard chicken raising. You can explore this option if you are seriously committed to owning your own chicken coop. Here are some tips that may help you along the way:

Find out the specificity of your local ordinances or laws. Some of them may be vague or may have loopholes that you can use to your advantage. A good example is a restriction on barn animals in general but not specifically on poultry.

Find out if anybody else has started an effort to change laws. You can create a support group and encourage other people to join in on your cause. With signatures, you can file a formal petition for the changes that you are commonly after.

Get your facts straight, make sure that you understand current laws and have explored all the conditions and clauses that make up that law. Find out the possibility of amending the conditions stated or of having a new ordinance promulgated.

Ask about policies in cities or localities that have less restrictive chicken laws and try to make a similar draft for an ordinance appropriate for your current location. Gather support for your cause and be as persistent as possible. After which you could contact your local government authorities about the protocols of public meetings and opportunities of submitting requests such as your own.

Expect the whole process to take time, even lasting up to a few months. Be courteous, respectful, and patient. The whole thing takes commitment and dedication. If you are really serious with your effort, then you can eventually expect results from all your hard work.

Chapter - 12
TIPS FOR RAISING CHICKENS

The way toward in raising chickens includes a lot of details that you should know in advance. It is critical to know about certain realities, so as to be able to raise your chickens without issues. Below are some valuable tips and recommendations that can assist you with raising your chickens with no issue.

First and foremost, it is imperative to plan what number of chickens you have to raise. Regardless of whether you are raising chickens for eggs or meats, the items can be in abundance on the off chance that you think little of your chicken's production power. For instance, four or five chickens are sufficient to cover your need for eggs lasting through the year. In the event that you raise ten chickens, at that point, you will have very numerous eggs for your needs.

Picking the right tools for your chickens is significant. Try not to go for cheap items that won't last long. It is vastly imperative to put resources into top-notch equipment that will assist you with producing more meat and eggs. It will give you an awesome incentive for your cash.

Chickens are sensitive. They are effectively influenced by climate conditions, so it is critical to ensure that the environment inside the coop is ideal for birds. Utilize a warming lamp to give additional glow inside the coop; yet don't think little of its capacity. It could negatively affect the chickens if the coop is overheated.

Food and water are fundamental for chickens. They can't withstand deficiency of water, so it is significant to screen the water dispenser and top them up as regularly as the feeders. Water will keep your chickens hydrated, so ensure that they get enough water with a decent-to-drink temperature. During winter, water can without much of a stretch transform into ice and this will make it incomprehensible for the chickens to drink, so ensure that you have water allocator warmer set up. It will keep the water in a decent condition for the chickens to drink.

One of the significant missteps that raisers/breeders make is to neglect to change the straw flooring now and again. The ground surface is a significant thing in the coop, and it ought to consistently stay dry and new. The nearness of water in the bedding will assist microorganisms to flourish and infect the chickens.

Top Five Things You Need to Be Aware of When Raising Chickens

There are various purposes behind raising your own chickens. Like other pet rearing, raising chickens has its own positive and negative sides. If you are new to raising chickens, you ought to find out about certain perspectives; for example, coop maintenance, feed, raising space and more. You are not advised to begin raising chickens without considering these variables. In spite of the fact that this isn't advanced science, you should figure out how things work. Below are five significant things that you should know about when raising chickens:

*Feed

*Space

*Breed

*Maintenance

*Security

Feed: Give them the best nourishments and enhancements since wellbeing matters! If you are very new to raising chicken and you don't have a clue what food to give, it is smarter to give them chicken feed that you can get from the neighborhood store. Likewise, make sure to supply sufficient measures of water that is perfect and free from pollutions. Chicks generally prefer to take water every time, as this helps them in keeping up their general wellbeing.

Space: Imagine how awful you feel in the event that you don't discover enough space to walk and unwind. This will be upsetting and irritating. You should know that it is the same with chickens. Give them enough space to wander around, with the goal that they can discover creepy crawlies and scratch about. The space you give ought to rely on the number of chicks you are willing to raise. For example, if you are raising three chicks, having thirty square feet of land will be sufficient for them to grow and roam.

Breed: Choosing the right breed is the essential factor that ought to be considered before you start raising chickens. Inspect your purposes for raising chickens. if it is only for eggs, pick a breed that can lay eggs in great numbers; if it is for meat, then you should find a breed that fulfills this kind of need.

Security: The most significant thing that you ought to never bargain with is security. Chicks are fragile and they can without much of a stretch be assaulted by vicious predators; for example, hawks and foxes. To shield your chickens from these animals, it is advisable to construct a coop where the chicks can live securely.

Maintenance matters a great deal. You should keep the chickens and their coop clean and shield them from diseases. Else, they can succumb to some infectious ailments.

Learn How to Raise Chickens Coming from Professional Chicken Breeders

Raising chickens is made simpler by pointers originating from proficient reproducers and raisers that are prepared to help in any capacity they need to. Truth be told, regardless of whether you are raising backyard chickens or raising them in a ranch, you should simply realize where to search for guides. Besides the general guides or manual on the best way to raise chickens, you can likewise search for approaches to maximize the yield of your chickens for greatest productivity.

Chickens find it quite easy to adapt to a little space where they can perch, peck, and eat conveniently. It is significant in realizing how to raise chickens that you know how to shield their eggs from being squashed in the coop. This is normally facilitated by gathering them promptly in the morning and figuring out how to move toward the coop calmly.

The coop is the place where the chickens lay their eggs, perch, seek shelter and go around for exercise. Consequently, the coop ought to give a decent safe haven for the chickens and free space to move around without stomping on one another. Ensure that the spot is free of parasites and different source of ailments that can hurt them. A well-depleted site is likewise prescribed for their simple access to a perfect and well-kept territory.

For chickens to flourish in any condition is reliant on the breed and on the age of the chickens. In figuring out how to raise chickens, you need to realize that the more youthful chickens are not as versatile as older chickens. In the event that you are in a region where the climate condition is erratic, make sure you raise chickens that can undoubtedly survive. Make a proper house for the chickens to the sort of climate in the zone. If the territory has a blistering atmosphere, you need to protect the chickens from the sun, or the chickens will experience dehydration and heat-empowered situations.

During hot climate, you can saturate the dirt with water, so it doesn't collect a lot of heat and become awkward for the chickens. There are guides on the most proficient method to raise chickens that will detail how to avoid exposure to the harsh elements and the outrageous heat.

Anyway, for a cold atmosphere, chickens that have a thick quill protection are appropriate. A rundown of the potential breeds is available.

Chickens additionally need a fix of dry land where you can nourish them. Feeds should be kept dry, so any feed that gives indications of clamminess and toxicity quality must be gotten rid of right away. For your chickens to survive, you should take very good care of them with every one of your available resources.

RAISE CHICKEN LIKE AN EXPERT!

So, you need to raise chickens, is that it? If you feel that it is a simple activity, maybe you have to think again. While they might be anything but difficult to raise, there are numerous things that you need to adapt first on the best way to raise chicken like a rancher would. Regardless of whether you might be raising lawn chickens or chickens on a ranch for whatever reason you may have, what is significant is to recall these basic pointers with the goal that you can unhesitatingly realize how to raise chicken.

There are not many things that you will require so as to be able to raise your first group of poultry. As a matter of first importance, think about the facilities or the living quarters of your chickens. It is essential to realize where to put the chicken coop as this will extraordinarily influence your chickens' development. Ensure that the territory is spotless and dry. Incorporate a home box for the hens that should perch around evening time. You can utilize a little piece of your garage or garden as the house for your chickens. The garden would be more fitting anyway, as chickens like to scratch on soil and uncover worms and bugs. Give them abundant space where they can likewise scratch on and still not demolish your garden patch.

The following stage or thing that is required on the most proficient method to raise chicken is its water and food. Much the same as any individual and creature, your chickens need to eat. There are a lot of pet stores that sell chicken feed or in the event that you need, you can likewise give them kitchen scraps like greens, bread, and fruit peelings. It is additionally imperative to give your chickens enough grit for them to process food.

The next basic is obviously, having to choose the correct hen to begin with. If you need to have the option to raise chicken for domesticated animals or eggs, at that point you will need to get either the bantams or the full-size hens. Bantams lay littler eggs compared with the full-size hens and are commonly noisier than the latter. It is intriguing to take note that there are additionally a few brands of hens and selecting the right one can represent the deciding moment of your venture on the most proficient method to raise chicken.

The most effective method to raise chicken is a truly productive undertaking. In addition to the fact that you are ready to accomplish something valuable, you are additionally ready to receive something in return simultaneously. For as long as you observe the essentials, you are well on your approach to effectively raise your first cluster of poultry.

Conclusions

Keeping chickens is a fantastic hobby and very rewarding. Hens make surprisingly good pets, are entertaining to watch and you get the benefit of fresh eggs too!

This isn't something you should just leap in to, but you need to plan and prepare. Reading this book is a good first step, and now you are aware of what you need for keeping hens.

Start by working out where you can keep your chickens in your garden and how much space they will have. Once this is done, measure up coops and runs, then you can determine exactly how many chickens you have the space to keep. Remember that they can live for a number of years so be prepared for a long-term commitment. Check with local zoning and planning laws as well as any HOA regulations as to whether you can keep chickens.

Before you even see a chicken, you need to get their home set up, predator proofed and buy all the equipment you need. This initial outlay will be quite significant, but afterward there is only feed and bedding costs plus occasional vet fees.

Predator proofing is absolutely vital as this is the main way you will lose members of your flock. Take the time to ensure the coop and run is predator proof before you introduce chickens to it as this work is much easier to do without chickens helping and escaping!

Choose your breed well based on the size bird you are after and the traits you want. Remember that some birds are good layers but poor meat birds, some are good all-rounders and others make great meat birds but produce few eggs. Avoid mixing breeds initially, and certainly never mix more aggressive breeds with more timid breeds as they will fight.

Check your chickens daily for signs of ill health. Like many prey animals, they are very good at hiding signs of illness, but you will learn to spot them and take the required early action to save them.

Ensure your chickens get the right food and regular treats. It will keep them healthy and happy, though avoid feeding them the foods which are bad for them or even poisonous to them. Check their run and around their living quarters regularly for any poisonous plants growing and remove them immediately.

So long as you provide your chickens with enough space to run around and roost, good nesting boxes and plenty of food, water, and grit, they will provide you with fresh eggs. Egg production falls when the weather gets cooler and stops during molting, but for much of the rest of the year you will get regular fresh eggs.

Whatever your plans for your chickens, whether eggs, meat or exhibiting, you will find that they are great animals to keep. They can be very sociable, and kids enjoy being involved in their upkeep. Be aware though that it is a significant time commitment as you need to visit your hens a minimum of twice a day, every day. This can make vacations difficult unless you can find a chicken sitter (try local keepers as they won't mind trading chicken sitting duties with you), but it is rewarding.

Printed in Great Britain
by Amazon

69242460R00050